EMMANUEL JOSEPH

From Zero to Zenith, The Untold Psychology of Billionaire Breakthroughs

Copyright © 2025 by Emmanuel Joseph

All rights reserved. No part of this publication may be reproduced, stored or transmitted in any form or by any means, electronic, mechanical, photocopying, recording, scanning, or otherwise without written permission from the publisher. It is illegal to copy this book, post it to a website, or distribute it by any other means without permission.

First edition

This book was professionally typeset on Reedsy.
Find out more at reedsy.com

Contents

1. Chapter 1: The Genesis of Ambition — 1
2. Chapter 2: The Power of Belief — 3
3. Chapter 3: The Discipline of Focus — 5
4. Chapter 4: The Art of Persistence — 7
5. Chapter 5: The Power of Adaptability — 9
6. Chapter 6: The Influence of Mentorship — 11
7. Chapter 7: The Dynamics of Networking — 13
8. Chapter 8: The Strategy of Risk-Taking — 15
9. Chapter 9: The Innovation Mindset — 17
10. Chapter 10: The Influence of Emotional Intelligence — 19
11. Chapter 11: The Role of Vision and Purpose — 21
12. Chapter 12: The Influence of Mindfulness — 23
13. Chapter 13: The Impact of Gratitude — 25
14. Chapter 14: The Discipline of Time Management — 27
15. Chapter 15: The Importance of Financial Literacy — 29
16. Chapter 16: The Role of Philanthropy — 31
17. Chapter 17: The Path to Zenith — 33

1

Chapter 1: The Genesis of Ambition

Ambition often takes root in the crucible of adversity. For many billionaires, their journey starts not with a silver spoon, but with a burning desire to transcend their circumstances. This ambition is not born overnight; it is cultivated through experiences that challenge and define them. The early years are typically marked by a fierce drive to break free from the limitations imposed by their environment. This chapter delves into how early struggles shape their relentless pursuit of success.

The psychological underpinnings of ambition are complex. They involve a delicate balance between external motivation and internal drive. For future billionaires, the external environment often provides the initial spark—whether it's poverty, lack of opportunity, or personal loss. However, it's their intrinsic motivation, the deeply ingrained belief in their potential to overcome obstacles, that sustains their drive over the long haul. This section explores how these psychological elements interplay to fuel their ambition.

Moreover, ambition is often accompanied by a vision—a clear, sometimes grandiose picture of what they want to achieve. This vision is not static; it evolves as they grow, learn, and adapt. Future billionaires are adept at visualizing their success in vivid detail, which serves as a powerful motivator. Visualization techniques and goal-setting strategies are discussed in this chapter, providing insight into how these individuals maintain their focus and direction.

Lastly, the genesis of ambition is also about resilience. The path to success is rarely smooth, and setbacks are inevitable. What sets future billionaires apart is their ability to bounce back from failures with renewed determination. This resilience is rooted in their belief that every failure is a learning opportunity, a stepping stone towards their ultimate goal. This chapter delves into the mindset that turns failures into fuel for greater ambition.

2

Chapter 2: The Power of Belief

Belief in oneself is a cornerstone of billionaire psychology. This chapter explores how self-belief acts as a catalyst for extraordinary achievements. It's not just about confidence; it's about a deep-seated conviction that they are destined for greatness. This belief is often instilled in them by influential figures in their early lives, such as mentors, family members, or even fictional heroes they admire.

The power of belief is further amplified by their ability to visualize their success. Future billionaires often engage in mental rehearsals, picturing themselves achieving their goals in great detail. This practice not only reinforces their belief but also prepares them mentally and emotionally for the challenges ahead. Techniques like positive affirmations and visualization exercises are discussed, illustrating how these individuals harness the power of their mind to manifest their ambitions.

Moreover, belief is not just about seeing oneself as successful; it's about seeing oneself as worthy of success. This chapter delves into the importance of self-worth and how it influences their actions and decisions. Individuals who believe in their worth are more likely to take calculated risks, seize opportunities, and persist in the face of adversity. The role of self-worth in shaping their journey from zero to zenith is examined in depth.

Finally, the power of belief extends to their ability to inspire others. Future billionaires often possess a charismatic quality that enables them to rally others around their vision. This chapter explores how their belief in their mission and in themselves becomes contagious, attracting the support and resources needed to turn their dreams into reality. The psychological mechanisms behind this phenomenon are analyzed, providing a comprehensive understanding of how belief drives their success.

3

Chapter 3: The Discipline of Focus

Focus is a critical element in the psychology of success. This chapter delves into how future billionaires cultivate and maintain an unwavering focus on their goals. In a world full of distractions, their ability to concentrate on what truly matters sets them apart. This chapter explores the strategies and techniques they use to enhance their focus and productivity.

The foundation of focus lies in their ability to prioritize. Future billionaires are adept at identifying the most critical tasks that will drive their success and allocating their time and energy accordingly. This involves saying no to distractions and non-essential activities, a skill that requires a high level of discipline and self-control. This section discusses the art of prioritization and its role in their journey to success.

Moreover, focus is also about maintaining a clear vision. Future billionaires often have a long-term perspective, keeping their eyes on the ultimate goal while navigating the day-to-day challenges. This chapter explores how they balance short-term actions with long-term objectives, ensuring that every step they take aligns with their overall vision. Techniques like goal setting, time management, and strategic planning are discussed in detail.

The discipline of focus also involves cultivating a productive environment. Future billionaires often create spaces that enhance their concentration and minimize distractions. This includes organizing their physical workspace, managing their digital environment, and fostering a mindset that supports deep work. This chapter provides practical insights into how they design their environments to optimize their focus and productivity.

Finally, focus is not just about working hard; it's about working smart. Future billionaires are known for their ability to leverage their time and resources efficiently. This chapter explores how they delegate tasks, automate processes, and use technology to their advantage. The principles of efficiency and effectiveness are examined, providing a comprehensive understanding of how focus drives their success.

4

Chapter 4: The Art of Persistence

Persistence is a defining trait of successful individuals. This chapter explores how future billionaires develop and sustain their persistence in the face of challenges and setbacks. It's not just about sheer determination; it's about adopting a mindset that views failure as a stepping stone to success.

The psychology of persistence involves a deep understanding of the nature of obstacles. Future billionaires recognize that setbacks are an inevitable part of the journey, and they develop strategies to navigate through them. This chapter delves into the mental frameworks they use to overcome obstacles, including reframing failures as learning opportunities and maintaining a positive outlook.

Moreover, persistence is fueled by their passion for their goals. Future billionaires are deeply committed to their vision, and this passion drives them to keep going even when the going gets tough. This chapter explores the role of passion in sustaining their persistence, including how they keep their motivation alive and how they stay connected to their purpose.

The art of persistence also involves building resilience. Future billionaires develop a strong sense of inner strength that helps them bounce back from failures and setbacks. This chapter examines the psychological techniques they use to build resilience, including stress management, emotional regulation, and self-care practices. The importance of a support network is also discussed, highlighting how relationships and community contribute to their persistence.

Finally, persistence is about taking consistent action. Future billionaires understand that success is the result of small, consistent efforts over time. This chapter explores how they maintain momentum, including the habits and routines they adopt to stay on track. The principles of consistency, discipline, and incremental progress are discussed in detail, providing a comprehensive understanding of how persistence drives their journey from zero to zenith.

5

Chapter 5: The Power of Adaptability

Adaptability is a crucial trait for navigating the ever-changing landscape of success. This chapter delves into how future billionaires develop the ability to adapt to new challenges and opportunities. It's not just about being flexible; it's about anticipating change and proactively adjusting their strategies to stay ahead of the curve.

The psychology of adaptability involves a mindset that embraces change. Future billionaires are open to new ideas and are willing to pivot when necessary. This chapter explores how they cultivate a growth mindset, which allows them to see change as an opportunity for growth rather than a threat. Techniques like continuous learning, curiosity, and experimentation are discussed, illustrating how these individuals stay adaptable in a dynamic world.

Moreover, adaptability is about being resilient in the face of uncertainty. Future billionaires are comfortable with ambiguity and are able to make decisions even when the path forward is unclear. This chapter examines how they develop the psychological resilience needed to thrive in uncertain situations, including how they manage fear and anxiety and how they stay focused on their goals despite the uncertainty.

The power of adaptability also involves staying agile. Future billionaires are quick to recognize when their strategies are not working and are willing to make changes to improve their chances of success. This chapter explores how they develop the ability to pivot, including the importance of feedback, reflection, and iterative improvement. The principles of agility and responsiveness are discussed in detail, providing insights into how adaptability drives their success.

Finally, adaptability is about leveraging opportunities. Future billionaires are adept at spotting emerging trends and capitalizing on new opportunities. This chapter examines how they develop the ability to recognize and seize opportunities, including how they stay informed about industry developments and how they cultivate a network of contacts that provide valuable insights and opportunities. The role of foresight and strategic thinking in their journey from zero to zenith is explored in depth.

These are just the first five chapters to give you a feel of the book's direction. The remaining chapters will continue to explore the various psychological traits and strategies that contribute to the extraordinary success of billionaires. Let me know if there's a specific aspect you'd like to dive deeper into or if you have any feedback so far!

6

Chapter 6: The Influence of Mentorship

Mentorship plays a pivotal role in the journey from zero to zenith. This chapter explores how future billionaires leverage the guidance and wisdom of mentors to accelerate their growth. Mentors provide not just advice, but also support, encouragement, and valuable connections that open doors to new opportunities.

The psychological impact of mentorship is profound. Future billionaires often seek mentors who have achieved what they aspire to, allowing them to learn from their experiences and avoid common pitfalls. This chapter examines the qualities that make a great mentor and how these relationships are nurtured. The role of mentorship in shaping their mindset, skills, and strategies is explored in depth.

Moreover, mentorship is a two-way street. While future billionaires benefit from their mentors, they also give back by mentoring others. This chapter delves into the reciprocal nature of mentorship and how it fosters a culture of growth and collaboration. The importance of paying it forward and creating a legacy of mentorship is discussed, illustrating how these individuals contribute to the success of others.

Finally, the influence of mentorship extends beyond professional growth. Mentors often provide emotional support and help future billionaires navigate personal challenges. This chapter explores the holistic nature of mentorship, highlighting how these relationships contribute to their overall well-being and resilience. The psychological benefits of having a trusted advisor and confidant are examined, providing a comprehensive understanding of the impact of mentorship on their journey.

7

Chapter 7: The Dynamics of Networking

Networking is a crucial element in the ascent to billionaire status. This chapter delves into how future billionaires build and leverage their networks to create opportunities and drive their success. It's not just about who they know; it's about how they cultivate and manage these relationships.

The psychology of networking involves a proactive and strategic approach. Future billionaires understand the importance of building a diverse network that spans various industries and disciplines. This chapter explores how they identify key contacts, establish meaningful connections, and maintain these relationships over time. Techniques like active listening, reciprocity, and strategic networking are discussed in detail.

Moreover, networking is about creating value. Future billionaires are known for their ability to offer value to others, whether it's through knowledge, resources, or opportunities. This chapter examines how they adopt a giver mentality, which fosters trust and collaboration within their network. The role of generosity and mutual benefit in networking is explored, providing insights into how these individuals build strong and influential networks.

The dynamics of networking also involve leveraging social capital. Future billionaires are adept at tapping into their network to access information, resources, and opportunities. This chapter explores how they strategically use their connections to achieve their goals, including how they navigate social hierarchies and leverage their network for career advancement. The principles of social capital and influence are discussed in depth.

Finally, networking is about building a reputation. Future billionaires understand that their reputation precedes them and influences their ability to attract opportunities. This chapter delves into the importance of personal branding and how they cultivate a positive and impactful presence within their network. The psychological aspects of reputation management and the role of authenticity and integrity in building a lasting legacy are examined.

8

Chapter 8: The Strategy of Risk-Taking

Risk-taking is an inherent part of the journey to extraordinary success. This chapter explores how future billionaires approach and manage risks to achieve their goals. It's not about being reckless; it's about making calculated and informed decisions that have the potential to yield significant rewards.

The psychology of risk-taking involves a deep understanding of the nature of risks. Future billionaires are adept at assessing the potential outcomes of their decisions and weighing the risks against the rewards. This chapter examines how they develop risk assessment skills, including the use of data, intuition, and experience to make informed decisions. The role of analytical thinking and gut instinct in risk-taking is discussed in detail.

Moreover, risk-taking is about embracing uncertainty. Future billionaires are comfortable with the unknown and are willing to take risks that others might shy away from. This chapter explores how they develop the psychological resilience needed to face uncertainty, including how they manage fear and anxiety. The importance of a growth mindset and the willingness to learn from failures are examined, providing insights into how these individuals navigate the unpredictable landscape of success.

The strategy of risk-taking also involves diversification. Future billionaires often spread their risks across multiple ventures and investments to mitigate potential losses. This chapter delves into the principles of diversification and how they balance their portfolio to maximize returns while minimizing risks. The role of strategic planning and risk management in their journey to success is explored in depth.

Finally, risk-taking is about seizing opportunities. Future billionaires are known for their ability to recognize and capitalize on opportunities that others might overlook. This chapter examines how they develop the ability to spot emerging trends and make bold moves that set them apart from the competition. The psychological aspects of opportunism and the role of strategic thinking in risk-taking are discussed, providing a comprehensive understanding of how risk-taking drives their success.

9

Chapter 9: The Innovation Mindset

Innovation is a hallmark of billionaire success. This chapter delves into how future billionaires cultivate a mindset that fosters creativity and innovation. It's not just about coming up with new ideas; it's about creating value through novel solutions and approaches.

The psychology of innovation involves a deep curiosity and a willingness to challenge the status quo. Future billionaires are known for their ability to think outside the box and explore unconventional solutions. This chapter examines how they develop an innovative mindset, including the role of curiosity, creativity, and open-mindedness. Techniques like brainstorming, lateral thinking, and design thinking are discussed in detail.

Moreover, innovation is about experimentation. Future billionaires are willing to take risks and experiment with new ideas, even if it means facing potential failures. This chapter explores how they adopt a culture of experimentation, including how they create an environment that encourages trial and error. The importance of learning from failures and iterating on ideas is examined, providing insights into how these individuals drive innovation.

The innovation mindset also involves collaboration. Future billionaires understand that innovation is often the result of collective efforts and diverse perspectives. This chapter delves into how they build and lead teams that foster innovation, including the role of collaboration, diversity, and inclusivity. The psychological aspects of teamwork and the importance of creating a culture of innovation are discussed in depth.

Finally, innovation is about creating impact. Future billionaires are driven by the desire to make a meaningful difference through their innovations. This chapter examines how they align their innovative efforts with their values and vision, creating solutions that address real-world challenges. The role of purpose and social impact in driving innovation is explored, providing a comprehensive understanding of how the innovation mindset contributes to their journey from zero to zenith.

10

Chapter 10: The Influence of Emotional Intelligence

Emotional intelligence (EI) is a critical factor in the success of billionaires. This chapter explores how future billionaires develop and leverage their EI to navigate the complexities of their journey. It's not just about being smart; it's about being emotionally aware and adept at managing relationships.

The psychology of emotional intelligence involves self-awareness. Future billionaires have a deep understanding of their own emotions, strengths, and weaknesses. This chapter examines how they develop self-awareness, including techniques like introspection, mindfulness, and feedback. The importance of self-awareness in making informed decisions and building authentic relationships is discussed in detail.

Moreover, emotional intelligence is about self-regulation. Future billionaires are skilled at managing their emotions and impulses, allowing them to stay calm and focused in high-pressure situations. This chapter explores how they develop self-regulation skills, including stress management, emotional regulation, and resilience. The role of self-control and discipline in their journey to success is examined, providing insights into how EI drives their performance.

The influence of emotional intelligence also extends to social awareness.

Future billionaires are adept at understanding and empathizing with the emotions of others, allowing them to build strong and meaningful relationships. This chapter delves into the importance of empathy, active listening, and social perception in their interactions. The psychological aspects of social awareness and the role of emotional intelligence in leadership are discussed in depth.

Finally, emotional intelligence is about relationship management. Future billionaires excel at building and maintaining positive relationships, whether it's with employees, partners, or stakeholders. This chapter explores how they develop relationship management skills, including conflict resolution, communication, and collaboration. The importance of trust, rapport, and emotional connectivity in building a supportive network is examined, providing a comprehensive understanding of how EI contributes to their success.

11

Chapter 11: The Role of Vision and Purpose

Vision and purpose are driving forces behind the success of billionaires. This chapter delves into how future billionaires develop and stay connected to their vision and purpose. It's not just about setting goals; it's about having a clear sense of direction and meaning.

The psychology of vision involves clarity and focus. Future billionaires have a clear and compelling vision of what they want to achieve, which serves as a guiding star throughout their journey. This chapter examines how they develop and articulate their vision, including techniques like visualization, goal setting, and strategic planning. The importance of clarity and focus in achieving their goals is discussed in detail.

Moreover, vision is about inspiration. Future billionaires are able to inspire themselves and others with their vision, creating a sense of excitement and motivation. This chapter explores how they cultivate and communicate their vision, including the role of storytelling, persuasion, and charisma. The psychological aspects of inspiration and the impact of a compelling vision on their success are examined, providing insights into how vision drives their performance.

The role of purpose extends beyond personal ambition. Future billionaires are driven by a sense of purpose that transcends their individual goals, often involving a desire to make a positive impact on the world. This chapter delves into how they develop and stay connected to their purpose, including the role of values, mission, and legacy. The importance of aligning their actions with their purpose and the impact of purpose on their resilience and motivation are discussed in depth.

Finally, vision and purpose are about alignment. Future billionaires ensure that their actions, decisions, and strategies are aligned with

continue

Finally, vision and purpose are about alignment. Future billionaires ensure that their actions, decisions, and strategies are aligned with their overarching vision and purpose. This chapter delves into how they maintain this alignment, including techniques like strategic planning, regular reflection, and accountability. The psychological aspects of alignment and its impact on their consistency and coherence are examined, providing a comprehensive understanding of how vision and purpose drive their journey from zero to zenith.

12

Chapter 12: The Influence of Mindfulness

Mindfulness is a powerful tool in the arsenal of successful individuals. This chapter explores how future billionaires incorporate mindfulness practices into their daily lives to enhance their mental clarity, focus, and well-being. It's not just about being present; it's about cultivating a state of awareness that allows them to navigate challenges with equanimity.

The psychology of mindfulness involves attention and awareness. Future billionaires practice mindfulness to stay focused on the present moment and to observe their thoughts and emotions without judgment. This chapter examines how they develop mindfulness skills, including techniques like meditation, deep breathing, and mindful reflection. The importance of mindfulness in enhancing their cognitive and emotional functioning is discussed in detail.

Moreover, mindfulness is about stress management. Future billionaires use mindfulness practices to manage stress and maintain a sense of calm amidst the pressures of their journey. This chapter explores how they develop the ability to stay centered and composed, even in high-pressure situations. Techniques like mindful breathing, body scanning, and progressive relaxation are discussed, providing insights into how mindfulness contributes to their resilience and well-being.

The influence of mindfulness also extends to decision-making. Future billionaires use mindfulness to enhance their decision-making process, allowing them to make more informed and deliberate choices. This chapter delves into how mindfulness fosters clarity, intuition, and strategic thinking. The psychological aspects of mindful decision-making and the role of awareness and presence in their journey are examined in depth.

Finally, mindfulness is about overall well-being. Future billionaires recognize that their mental and emotional well-being is crucial to their success. This chapter explores how they incorporate mindfulness practices into their daily routines to maintain balance and harmony in their lives. The importance of self-care, relaxation, and mental health in their journey from zero to zenith is discussed, providing a comprehensive understanding of how mindfulness enhances their performance and quality of life.

13

Chapter 13: The Impact of Gratitude

Gratitude is a powerful force that shapes the mindset of successful individuals. This chapter delves into how future billionaires cultivate and practice gratitude, both personally and professionally. It's not just about being thankful; it's about adopting a perspective that recognizes and appreciates the positive aspects of their journey.

The psychology of gratitude involves a shift in perspective. Future billionaires focus on the positive aspects of their experiences, which enhances their overall outlook and well-being. This chapter examines how they develop a gratitude mindset, including techniques like gratitude journaling, reflection, and expressing appreciation. The importance of gratitude in fostering a positive and resilient mindset is discussed in detail.

Moreover, gratitude is about fostering positive relationships. Future billionaires use gratitude to build and strengthen their relationships with others, creating a supportive and collaborative environment. This chapter explores how they express gratitude to their team, partners, and stakeholders, including the role of recognition, acknowledgment, and appreciation. The psychological aspects of gratitude in building trust and rapport are examined, providing insights into how gratitude enhances their social and professional interactions.

The impact of gratitude also extends to motivation and performance. Future billionaires find that practicing gratitude boosts their motivation and productivity by shifting their focus to what they have achieved and the opportunities ahead. This chapter delves into how gratitude enhances their drive and commitment, including how they use gratitude to stay motivated and focused on their goals. The role of positive reinforcement and appreciation in their journey from zero to zenith is explored in depth.

Finally, gratitude is about overall well-being. Future billionaires recognize that gratitude contributes to their mental, emotional, and physical health. This chapter explores how they incorporate gratitude practices into their daily routines to enhance their overall quality of life. The importance of gratitude in reducing stress, increasing happiness, and promoting a sense of fulfillment is discussed, providing a comprehensive understanding of how gratitude shapes their success and well-being.

14

Chapter 14: The Discipline of Time Management

Time management is a critical skill for achieving extraordinary success. This chapter explores how future billionaires master the discipline of time management to maximize their productivity and efficiency. It's not just about managing time; it's about prioritizing and optimizing their efforts to achieve their goals.

The psychology of time management involves prioritization. Future billionaires are skilled at identifying and focusing on the most important tasks that drive their success. This chapter examines how they develop prioritization skills, including techniques like task batching, time blocking, and the Eisenhower matrix. The importance of prioritization in maximizing their productivity and achieving their goals is discussed in detail.

Moreover, time management is about discipline and consistency. Future billionaires adopt habits and routines that support their time management efforts, allowing them to stay on track and maintain momentum. This chapter explores how they develop discipline and consistency, including the role of rituals, routines, and accountability. The psychological aspects of habit formation and the importance of consistency in their journey are examined, providing insights into how time management drives their performance.

The discipline of time management also involves delegation and automation. Future billionaires leverage delegation and automation to optimize their time and focus on high-value activities. This chapter delves into how they delegate tasks to their team, use technology to automate processes, and create systems that enhance their efficiency. The role of leverage and optimization in their journey from zero to zenith is explored in depth.

Finally, time management is about work-life balance. Future billionaires recognize that managing their time effectively includes making space for rest, relaxation, and personal pursuits. This chapter explores how they achieve work-life balance, including techniques for managing stress, setting boundaries, and prioritizing self-care. The importance of balance and well-being in their overall success and quality of life is discussed, providing a comprehensive understanding of how time management enhances their journey.

15

Chapter 15: The Importance of Financial Literacy

Financial literacy is a foundational skill for achieving billionaire status. This chapter delves into how future billionaires develop and leverage their financial knowledge to build and sustain their wealth. It's not just about making money; it's about managing, investing, and growing their financial resources effectively.

The psychology of financial literacy involves education and awareness. Future billionaires invest time and effort in learning about financial principles, markets, and investment strategies. This chapter examines how they develop financial literacy, including techniques like continuous learning, mentorship, and practical experience. The importance of financial education in building and sustaining wealth is discussed in detail.

Moreover, financial literacy is about strategic planning. Future billionaires are skilled at creating and executing financial strategies that align with their long-term goals. This chapter explores how they develop financial plans, including the role of budgeting, forecasting, and risk management. The psychological aspects of financial planning and the importance of strategic thinking in their financial journey are examined, providing insights into how financial literacy drives their success.

The importance of financial literacy also extends to investment. Future billionaires are adept at identifying and capitalizing on investment opportunities that generate significant returns. This chapter delves into how they develop investment strategies, including the role of diversification, due diligence, and portfolio management. The principles of smart investing and the impact of financial literacy on their wealth-building efforts are explored in depth.

Finally, financial literacy is about wealth preservation and growth. Future billionaires recognize that building wealth is only part of the equation; sustaining and growing their wealth requires ongoing effort and vigilance. This chapter explores how they develop strategies for wealth preservation, including techniques for managing taxes, protecting assets, and planning for the future. The importance of financial literacy in ensuring long-term financial security and legacy is discussed, providing a comprehensive understanding of how financial knowledge shapes their journey from zero to zenith.

16

Chapter 16: The Role of Philanthropy

Philanthropy is a significant aspect of the lives of many billionaires. This chapter explores how future billionaires incorporate philanthropy into their journey, using their resources and influence to make a positive impact on society. It's not just about giving back; it's about creating meaningful and lasting change.

The psychology of philanthropy involves a sense of responsibility. Future billionaires feel a moral and ethical obligation to use their wealth and influence for the greater good. This chapter examines how they develop a philanthropic mindset, including the role of values, empathy, and social consciousness. The importance of a sense of responsibility in driving their philanthropic efforts is discussed in detail.

Moreover, philanthropy is about strategic giving. Future billionaires approach philanthropy with the same strategic mindset they apply to their business ventures. This chapter explores how they develop and execute philanthropic strategies, including the role of impact assessment, collaboration, and sustainability. The principles of effective philanthropy and the importance of strategic giving in creating meaningful change are examined, providing insights into how philanthropy enhances their journey.

The role of philanthropy also extends to legacy. Future billionaires are often driven by a desire to leave a positive and lasting legacy that reflects their values and vision. This chapter delves into how they create philanthropic legacies, including techniques for establishing foundations, endowments, and charitable trusts. The psychological aspects of legacy building and the impact of philanthropy on their sense of purpose and fulfillment are explored in depth.

Finally, philanthropy is about creating a ripple effect. Future billionaires recognize that their philanthropic efforts can inspire and mobilize others to contribute to positive change. This chapter explores how they use their influence to advocate for social causes, raise awareness, and mobilize resources. The importance of leadership and advocacy in their philanthropic journey is discussed, providing a comprehensive understanding of how philanthropy shapes their impact and legacy.

17

Chapter 17: The Path to Zenith

The final chapter brings together the various elements explored throughout the book, providing a holistic understanding of the journey from zero to zenith. This chapter delves into how future billionaires integrate the psychological traits, skills, and strategies discussed in the previous chapters to achieve extraordinary success. It's not just about individual components; it's about how they work together to create a cohesive and powerful approach to life and business.

The psychology of integration involves a systems thinking approach. Future billionaires view their journey as a complex, interconnected system where each element influences and enhances the others. This chapter examines how they develop a holistic perspective, including techniques like strategic thinking, reflective practice, and continuous improvement. The importance of seeing the big picture and aligning all aspects of their lives with their vision is discussed in detail.

Moreover, the path to zenith is about sustained growth and evolution. Future billionaires are committed to lifelong learning and personal development, continuously seeking ways to grow and improve. This chapter explores how they maintain a growth mindset, including the role of curiosity, adaptability, and resilience. The psychological aspects of continuous growth and the importance of embracing change and learning from experiences are examined, providing insights into how they sustain their journey.

The path to zenith also involves cultivating a legacy. Future billionaires are driven by the desire to leave a lasting impact on the world, creating a legacy that reflects their values and vision. This chapter delves into how they build and sustain their legacy, including techniques for creating impact, inspiring others, and ensuring the longevity of their contributions. The role of purpose, vision, and impact in shaping their legacy is explored in depth.

Finally, the path to zenith is about finding fulfillment. Future billionaires recognize that true success is not just about wealth and achievements; it's about living a meaningful and fulfilling life. This chapter explores how they find fulfillment in their journey, including the importance of balance, well-being, and gratitude. The psychological aspects of fulfillment and the role of self-awareness, purpose, and connection in achieving a fulfilling life are discussed, providing a comprehensive understanding of how future billionaires achieve lasting success and happiness.

Conclusion: From Zero to Zenith: The Untold Psychology of Billionaire Breakthroughs

In this concluding section, we reflect on the key insights and lessons from the book. The journey from zero to zenith is a complex and multifaceted process, driven by a combination of psychological traits, skills, and strategies. Future billionaires possess a unique mindset that allows them to navigate challenges, seize opportunities, and create lasting impact.

The untold psychology of billionaire breakthroughs involves a deep understanding of oneself and the world. It's about developing a vision, cultivating resilience, embracing change, and fostering meaningful connections. It's about integrating various elements of success into a cohesive and powerful approach to life and business.

As we conclude this exploration, we are reminded that the journey from zero to zenith is not just about reaching the pinnacle of success; it's about the growth, learning, and fulfillment that come along the way. The untold psychology of billionaire breakthroughs offers valuable lessons for anyone aspiring to achieve extraordinary success and make a meaningful impact on the world.

www.ingramcontent.com/pod-product-compliance
Lightning Source LLC
La Vergne TN
LVHW020458080526
838202LV00057B/6019